# THE ADVENTURES OF
# BAMBINO

Dr Cypher

## BAMBINO GETS INTO MISCHIEF

## Thomas Jude Cypher

Xulon
ELITE

# Acknowledgements

**The Lord, The Almighty**- I want to thank Our Heavenly Father for the inspiration and wisdom to write this book. May The Lord's love, mercy, and forgiveness be evident to all who read this story, to the glory of Jesus Christ.

**Janet, my wife ("Mama")-** You are my soul mate and best friend! You have influenced every page. Thank you for your infinite love and confidence in me. You inspire me to excellence.

**My children (the "Family")-** You are 4 of our most precious gifts! Thank you for all of your wonderful contributions to this story!

**Amy Sheridan**- Thank you for your emotional insight. Your suggestions helped to put the heart into this story.

**Marilyn Howard**- Thank you for your Godly mentoring and guidance. Your generous advice and expert recommendations have blessed this entire project!

**William A. Langley**- Thank you for using your artistic vision to create images that can tell the story without using words.

**Bambino ("the Poochini")-** We thank The Lord for bringing you into our family (even if sometimes you are a little scaramouch).

# Words to Learn:

**Mischief**- Naughty behavior.

**Temptation**- A desire for something wrong.

**Sacrifice**- Giving-up something to honor and please God.

**Sinister**- Related to evil.

**Confess**- To admit and be sorry for doing wrong.

**Forgive**- Pardoning a mistake or wrongdoing.

**Scaramouch** (*scare-uh-mooch*)- A rascal.

Bambino is a puppy
Who loves to run and play,
And if he had his way
He would run and play all day.

One day, his family went shopping.
The store was not very far,
But the day was sunny and hot
So he could not wait in the car.

Mama said, "Bambino,
It's safer for you at home.
We promise to be back soon
Since you don't like being alone."

Bambino sat by the window,
And watched them drive down the street.
He thought, "I hope they remember
To bring home my favorite treat!"

As he gazed out the window
Bambino was able to see
Other dogs in the neighborhood
Playing so happy and free.

He waited what seemed like hours,
While his family was away.
He thought, "I hope they come home soon
So I can go out and play."

He trotted down to the kitchen.
Surprised, he noticed the door
Was accidentally left open.
"That's never happened before!"

He opened the kitchen door wider
By using the side of his nose,
But then Bambino realized
The screen door was tightly closed.

Bambino looked up at the handle.
He thought for a moment or two,
"I've seen my family open this door
And I know just what to do."

"If I jump as high as I can
And pull the handle down,
The door will open and I can play!"
Thought the clever little hound.

So Bambino jumped and jumped
And quickly got the door open.
He ran outside to join his friends
Just like he was hopin'.

He heard his friends at the pond,
So Bambino did not delay.
He ran as fast as he could,
"I finally get to play!"

All his friends were excited.
They splashed and enjoyed their swim.
Bambino thought, "It looks so fun!
I can't wait to jump-in!"

As Bambino was ready to jump,
He remembered his family said,
"Don't swim in the pond, Bambino."
He heard their words in his head,

"Bambino, stay out of the pond,
The water is not very clean.
Something grows on the surface
And turns the water green."

"There's also a poisonous snake
That lives at the edge of the pond.
He slithers and hides in the grass,
Around the water and beyond."

Bambino remembered their words
And the little pup seemed confused.
He wanted to obey his family
But his friends were very amused.

"Bambino, come in for a swim!
Be part of our happy crowd!"
He said, "I want to join in,
But my family said I'm not allowed!"

"You're not allowed?" they laughed,
And all of his friends gave a shout,
"We'll be done before they get home!
Your family will never find out!"

Temptation then lied to Bambino.
It urged him to disobey,
And as he tried hard to resist
He heard temptation say,

"Just go for a swim, Bambino,
It won't hurt anyone.
Do you really think your family
Doesn't want you having fun?"

Bambino paused for a moment,
"That doesn't sound so bad.
My family likes when I'm happy.
They don't want me to be sad."

So Bambino obeyed temptation
Instead of his family's advice.
Temptation gets you in trouble.
It's better to sacrifice.

Bambino jumped in the pond,
He splashed and had a great time,
And when he came out of the water
His fur was covered with slime!

Bambino knew that his family
Would realize he disobeyed!
He asked his friends to help him
But no one came to his aid.

Bambino shook and shook.
He rolled upon the ground.
As he tried to clean his fur,
He heard a hissing sound.

"You ssseem upsssset. Are you ok?
Isss there sssomething I can do?
My name iss ssSinister  ssSnake,
How can I asssist you?"

Bambino said, "I need your help!
Look at the mess I've made!
If I don't get this green stuff off
They'll know I disobeyed!"

Sinister said, "Come clossser,
You have nothing to fear.
I'll clean you up ssso that it looksss
Like you were never here!"

Sinister opened wide his mouth,
So that his fangs would show.
Then he lunged and tried to bite
Poor little Bambino!

Bambino jumped and
dodged the bite!
Sinister Snake just hissed!
Sinister Snake was angry
Because he barely missed.

Bambino turned and ran away!
He ran to the kitchen door,
Glad to see that his family
Had returned home from the store.

He barked and scratched the door.
He wanted to get in.
He knew he would be safe because
His family protected him.

He was happy to see Mama,
Who always loves and cares,
But when she let him
in the house
He became a little scared.

He thought, "I am in trouble!
They all will be upset!
I know that I deserve
Whatever punishment I get."

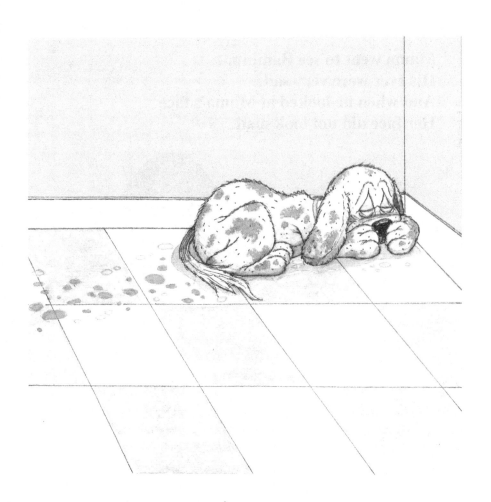

"How can I say 'I'm sorry',
And how can I confess?
How can I let my family know
I'm sorry for this mess?"

With his tail between his legs,
He walked slowly from the door.
He sadly went to the corner
And he curled-up on the floor.

Mama went to see Bambino.
His eyes were very sad,
And when he looked at Mama's face
Her face did not look mad.

She gently looked into his eyes
And said, "You disobeyed,
But we accept your apology.
You don't have to be afraid."

"You surrendered to temptation
And there's no one else to blame,
But we forgive you, Bambino.
There's no need to feel ashamed."

"We know that you are sorry.
We know that your heart aches,
But our love for you is greater
Than all of your mistakes."

So Mama called the family
And they came to see the pooch.
With his green and dirty fur,
He looked like a scaramouch.

His family said, "Bambino,
Your fur is green and stiff!
Did you go in the pond today
And get into some mischief?"

Bambino grinned a little grin.
His family was not mad.
He knew they all forgave him.
This made Bambino glad!

The family picked-up Bambino
And carried him to the tub.
They showered him with soap and water.
They showered him with love.

He fell asleep upon the couch
A clean and happy pup.
So pleased his family loves him still,
And forgives him…no matter what.

# The End

*Blessed are those whose disobedience is forgiven
and whose sins are pardoned.
(Romans 4:7, Psalm 32:1)*

# Bambino's Lessons

**Mercy**- Mercy is receiving compassion when you deserve punishment. Bambino deserved to be punished for disobeying, but he received mercy instead. Mercy does not give you permission to disobey. However, when you are truly sorry like Bambino, God's shows you mercy (Daniel 9:9, Luke 6:36).

**Forgiveness**- Because God loves you so much, He wants to forgive you for your sin. It is best not to sin, but if you disobey like Bambino, God and your family still love you. They will quickly forgive when you say you are sorry. (Psalm 86:5, Ephesians 4:32)

**Confession**- When you do something wrong, you must admit it. You must also say you are sorry to God and to the people you hurt. Confessing and repenting for your disobedience heals your friendship with God and restores your relationship with the people you hurt. (Psalm 32:5, 1 John1:9)

**Obedience**- The Bible says it is best to obey God and your parents. Like Bambino, even good boys and girls sometimes disobey. Whenever you are tempted to disobey, ask God to step between you and the temptation. God is faithful. When you ask God to get involved, He gives you the strength to resist temptation and do what pleases Him. (1 Kings 2:3, Ephesians 6:1-3)

CPSIA information can be obtained
at www.ICGtesting.com
Printed in the USA
BVOW10s1727240717

489977BV00003B/10/P